ANIMAL 173

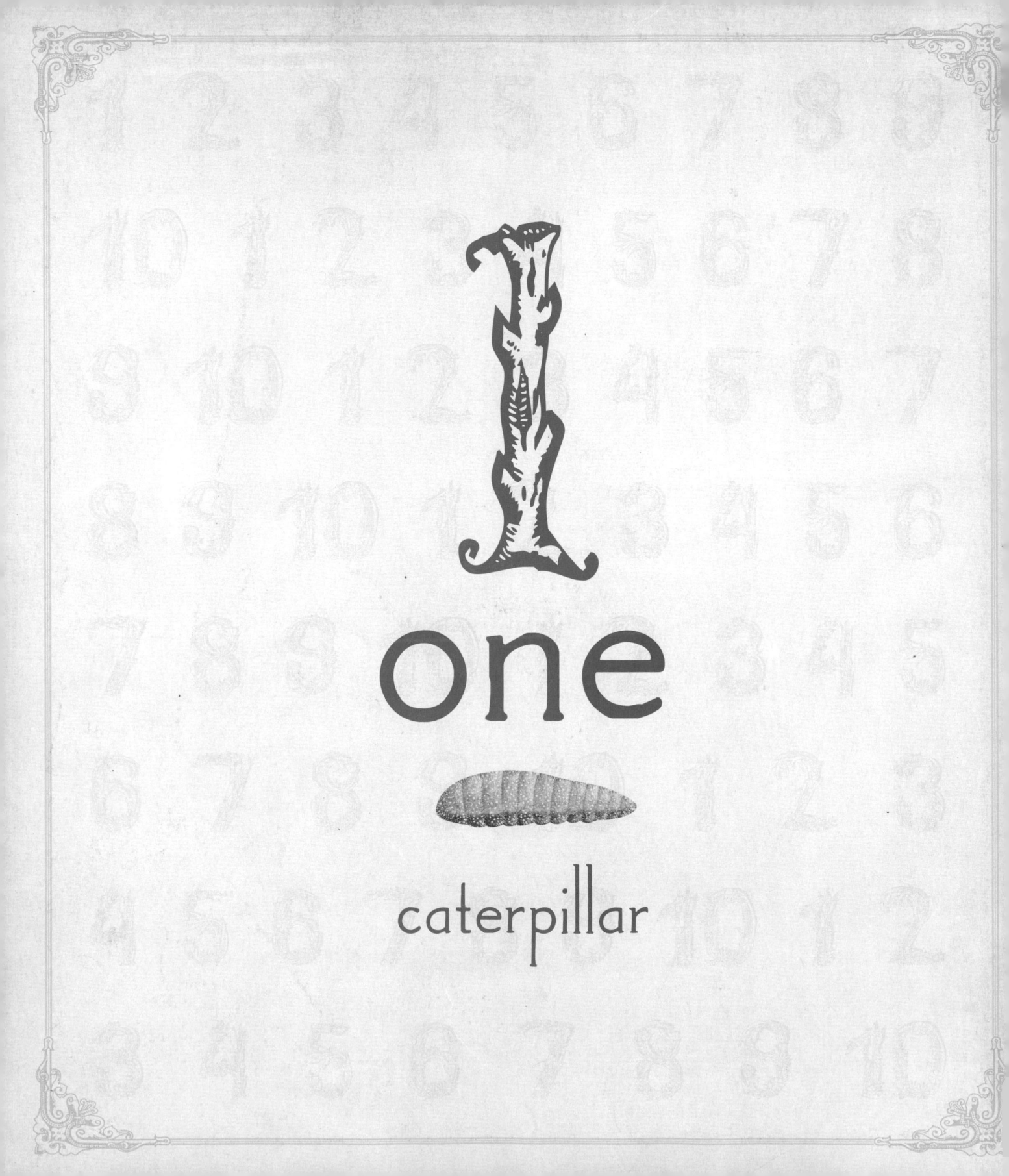

1
one

caterpillar

two parrots

three foxes

3

four bears

five whales

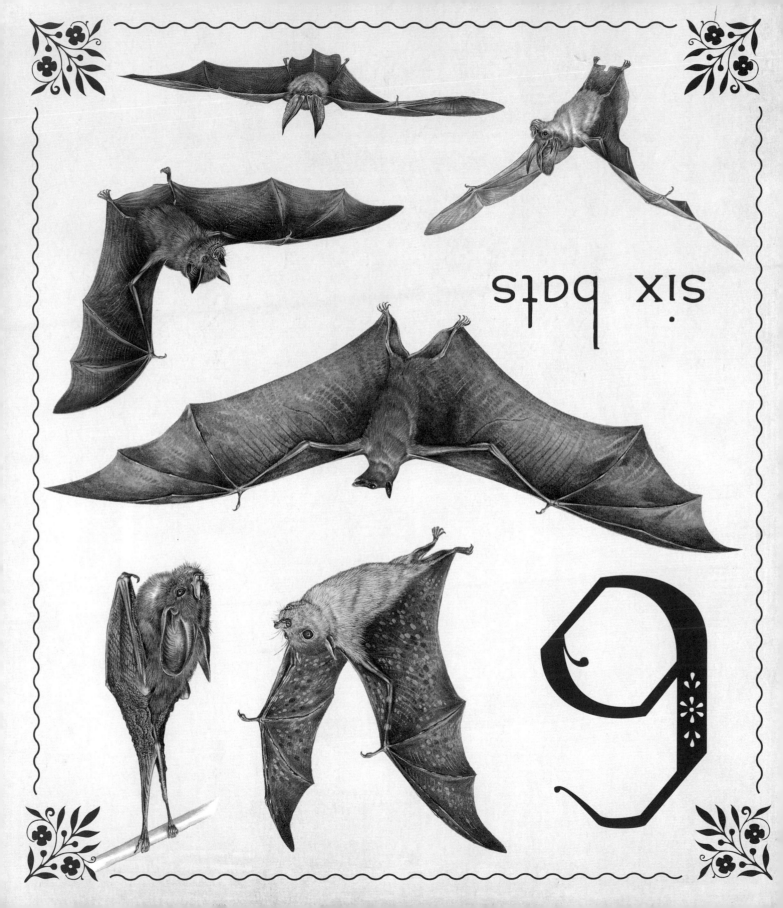

six bats

9

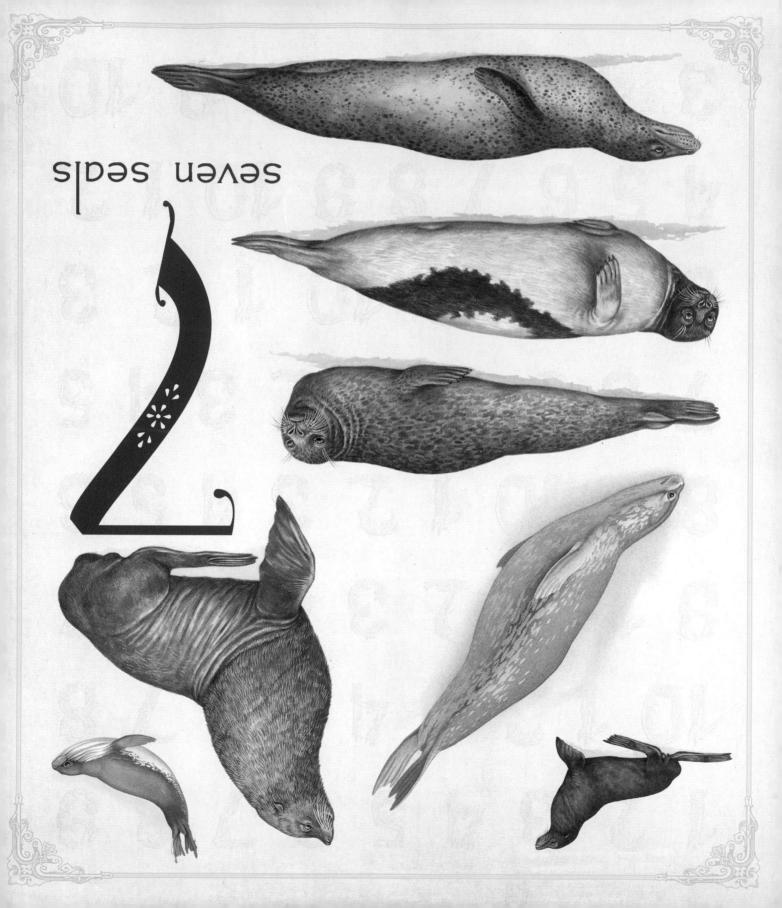

seven seals

2

eight salamanders

nine beavers

ten spiders

10

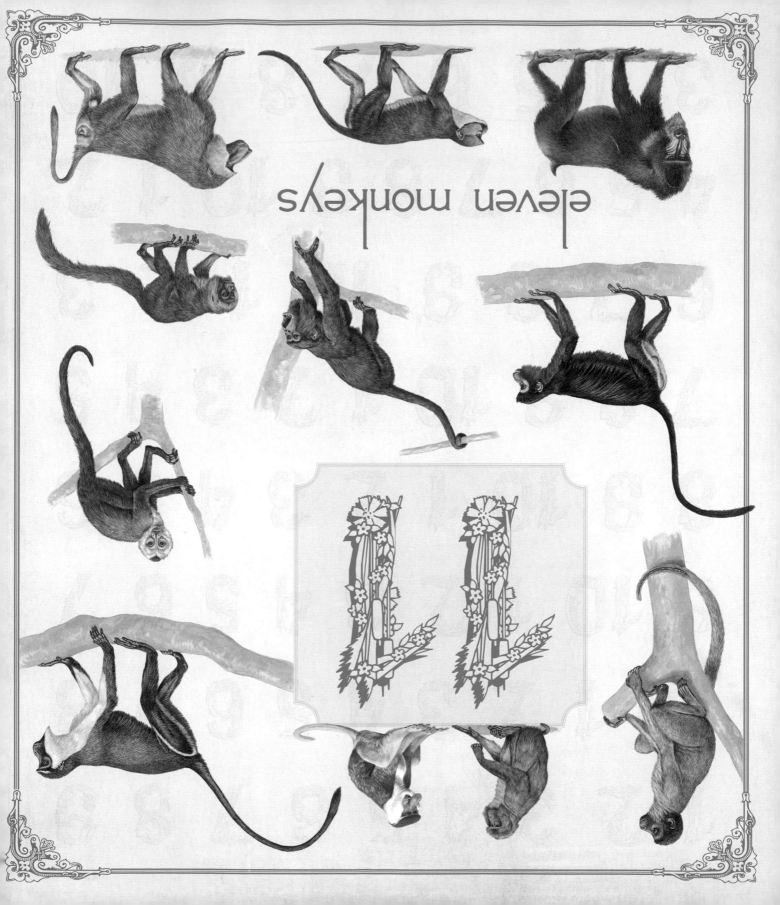

eleven monkeys

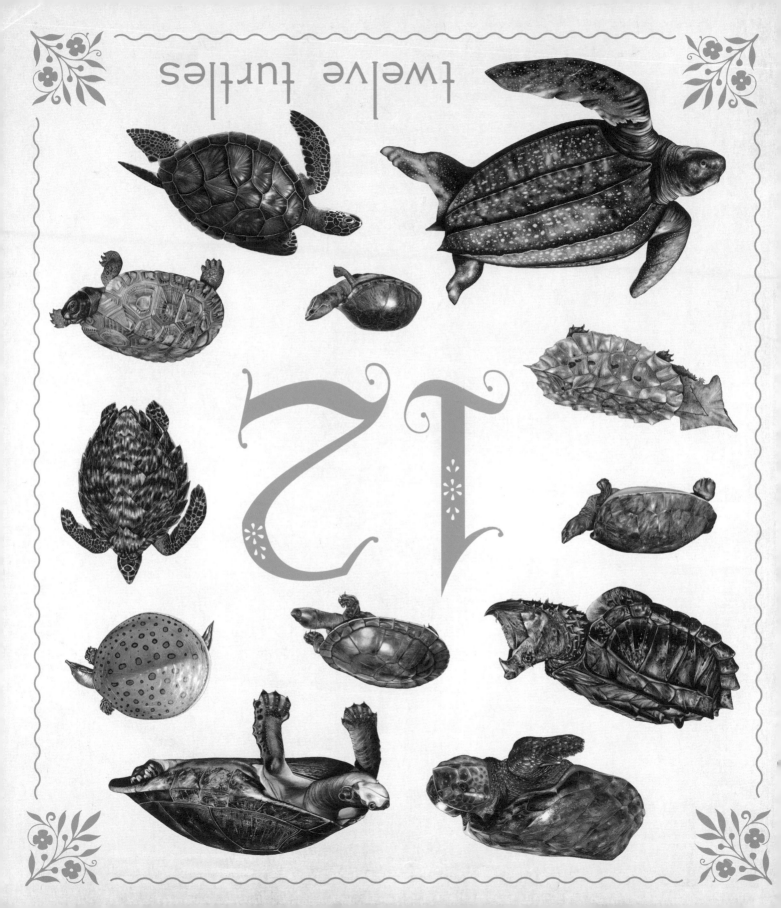

twelve turtles

12

thirteen lizards

13

14

fourteen tigers

fifteen snakes

15

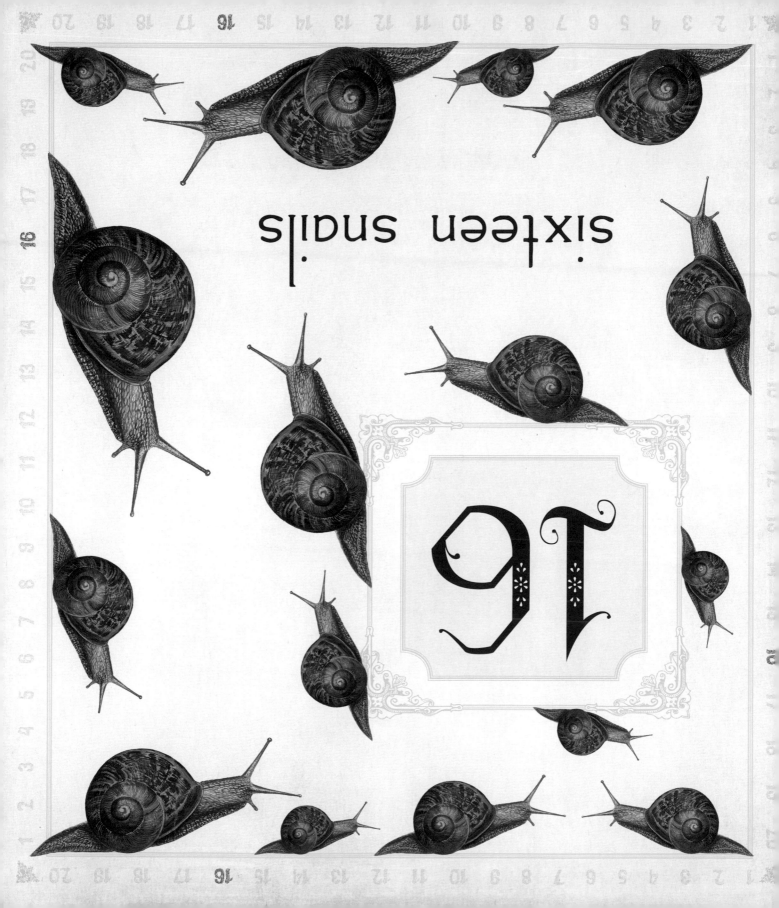

sixteen snails

16

seventeen beetles

17

eighteen birds

nineteen seahorses

twenty frogs

20

30

thirty flies

40

forty shrimps

fifty butterflies

50

sixty starfish

09

seventy mice

02

eighty ladybugs

08

ninety penguins

one hundred fish

100

A FIREFLY BOOK

Published by Firefly Books Ltd. 2014

First printing

Publisher Cataloging-in-Publication Data (U.S.)

Martin, Susi.
Animal 123 / Susi Martin.
 [32] pages ; col. photos. ; cm.
Summary: An introduction to counting and the animal kingdom through a menagerie of illustrations including birds and beetles, fish and fowl, and finishes with 100 fish to count. Features every number from 1 to 20, then in 10s to 100.
ISBN: 978-1-77085-454-3
 1. Counting – Juvenile literature. 2. Animals – Juvenile literature. I. Title.
513.211 [E] dc23 QA113.M368 2014

Library and Archives Canada Cataloguing in Publication

Martin, Susi, author
 Animal 123 / Susi Martin.
ISBN 978-1-77085-454-3 (bound)
 1. Counting – Juvenile literature. 2. Picture books for children. I. Title.
QA113.M365 2014   j513.2'11   C2014-901870-3

Published in the United States by
Firefly Books (U.S.) Inc.
P.O. Box 1338, Ellicott Station
Buffalo, New York 14205

Published in Canada by
Firefly Books Ltd.
50 Staples Avenue, Unit 1
Richmond Hill, Ontario L4B 0A7

Designed and edited by Tall Tree Ltd

Printed in China